LETTER FROM THE EDITORS

     The injustices that have occurred in the past and their rippling effects in our present are the focus of this month's issue. LET THEM EAT SHIT are words that may not have been literally thrown at us, but they have been sugar coated with side eye glances filled with disgust, unsolicited advice on how, and sometimes what language, to speak.

     People who are bathed in privilege are too often blind to realize or don't care to see how these hurtful words and actions affect and continue to mark their place in our present. In this issue, we have crafted responses for these people, the ones that stuff their faces with false kindness while stabbing us in the back with their hateful actions. Our responses are diverse like our backgrounds, rich like our cultures and painfully true like our current reality.

     From trying to comprehend why someone would be ashamed of their beautiful background to calling out people who use slurs without a blink of an eye. These stories and responses must be told. Between us this is known, but it's rarely known among the privileged. We hope that once you read through this issue, you'll also understand and feel the pain that each and everyone of us have felt when a LET THEM EAT SHIT mentality has been used to direct ignorance and hate toward us. Once you understand and see the result of these vile words, you can begin to be less of a blinded Marie Antoinette and more of an empathetic being.

     Through the voices of the marginalized, the outcasts and the ignored, we hope to start a dialogue. We hope to break down this us vs. them mentality. In a world that aspires to normalcy, to create and colonize the concept of being the average being, we have brought together a group of people that show us another way of thinking about the collective body of humanity. We hope that through the different lives and talents on these pages, you'll gather with us to deconstruct this pursuit of normalcy to replace it with an overwhelming acceptance of our differences. There is no better revenge, no better way to tell our oppressors to eat shit.

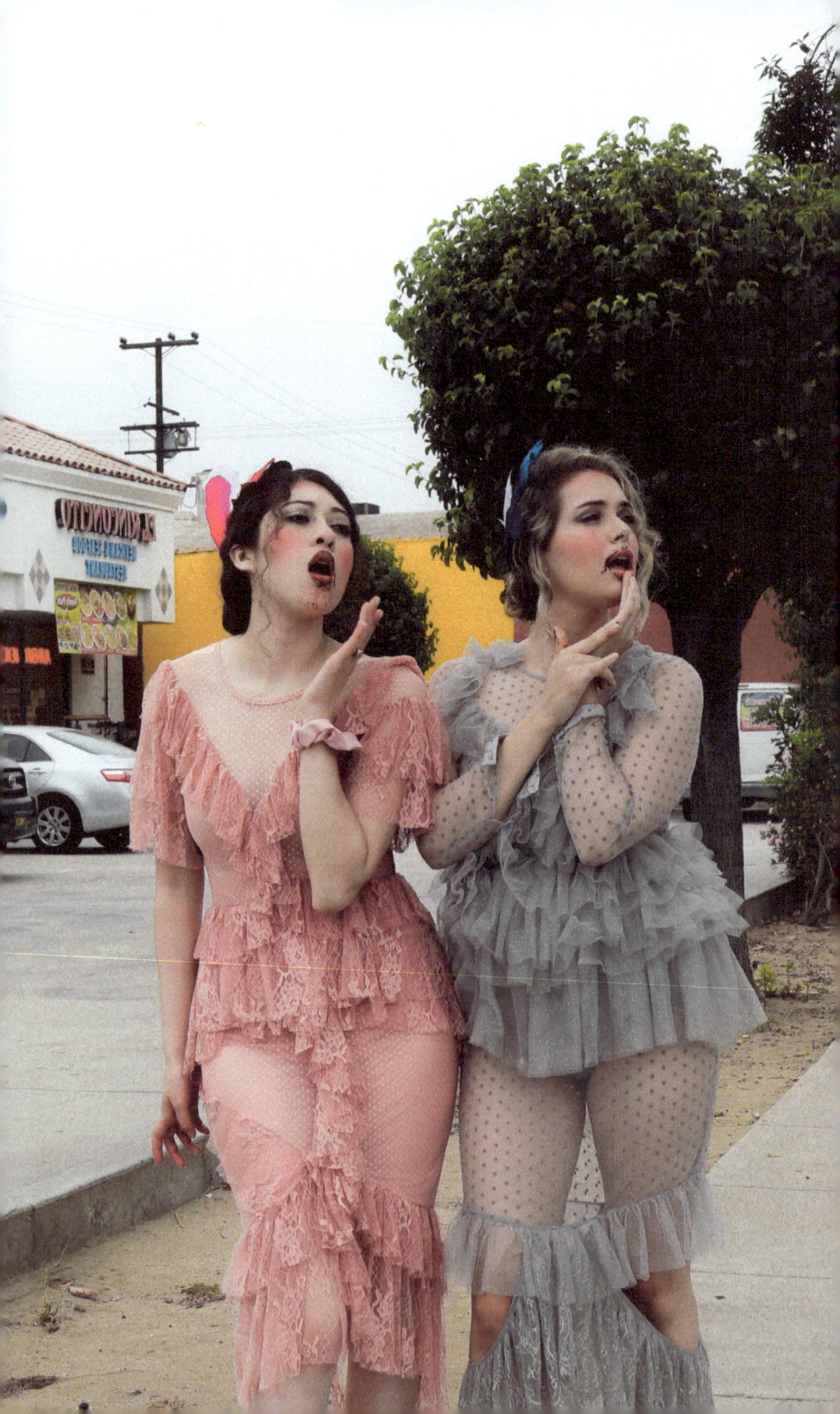

THIS MONTH

4	ERIC'S PEOPLE PROBLEM
7	THE SHIT THEY ROT IN
11	CRACKED
12	HIS PEOPLE
17	UNTITLED
18	LOVE IN THE AGE OF CONVENIENCE
19	FAKE GRASS BABE
23	DINNERS: DREW & LOGAN
24	TRACK TWO.
25	PARA MI MAMÁ Y MI ABUELA
29	PRETTY PEOPLE DIE IN LA
31	THE ANSWER TO THE PROBLEM

ERIC'S PEOPLE PROBLEM

JOSE CORDOVA

"When they piss and shit in the bushes, are they marking their territory?" Eric was looking out his balcony atop one of the city's most iconic buildings.

"Yes sir, that's what animals do. Vile things. If only they had the capacity to think like us, then maybe we'd have a stronger society." The polished brass on Mike's uniform gleamed even in the moonlight.

"You're god damned right. Well, being that you're so good with numbers, how many of these creatures are plaguing the river and train tracks? There's too many of them and we can't have that filth on display like that." Eric said.

"According to our estimates, there are sixty-five thousand of these god damned rats on the streets. Seventeen thousand of them have been camping along the river and tracks. At this rate, we'll have another eight to ten thousand joining them by Christmas. And with the lack of projected rain from now til next fall, you can be assured the number will double by then." Mike was definitely good with numbers.

"How do they multiply? Do these fuckers lay eggs? Can we exterminate their nests?" Eric said, spitting on the floor in disgust.

"Uh, sir, these creatures don't lay eggs. They almost replicate like we do, but faster."

"Give me the numbers Mike. How many can you get rid of by the end of next quarter? And I don't mean locked up in the pens you like to play with them in, I mean exterminate. We must thin them out before the Summer Games, I am not being embarrassed when company arrives. Your ass is on the line here Mike." Eric's thick eyebrows almost leaped off his head. This was an order that Mike knew was coming when he was summoned to the office.

"We can begin the process by week's end sir. It will take us 12 weeks, but by god we will have cleaned them all out by then. We can even speed up the process if you let us use the pineapples sir." Mike's chin raised slightly. He was ready, and damned happy he had that card to play.

"Where the hell you get grenades from? Who am I kidding, fuck it, go ahead and use them! I'll call the stadiums and have fireworks sponsored by us. Hell, you think we can get the Blue Angels to fly by and make some booms happen?" The long slender fingers of Eric's hand stroked his chin, he really liked the Blue Angels.

"Sir, that's absolutely brilliant!"

"Yes... Well now that we have that sorted out, I'm hungry. Wanna get some steaks?" His trademark smile had returned. The same smile he gave to all the photographers and at all his appearances. They always ate that shit up.

"Of course, sir."

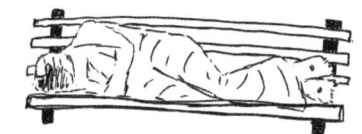

"I TELL YOU THE TRUTH, WHATEVER YOU DID TO THE LEAST OF THESE, YOU WERE DOING IT TO ME."
-MATTHEW 25:40

Jesus, the Homeless
Ink on paper *by Lex Brown*

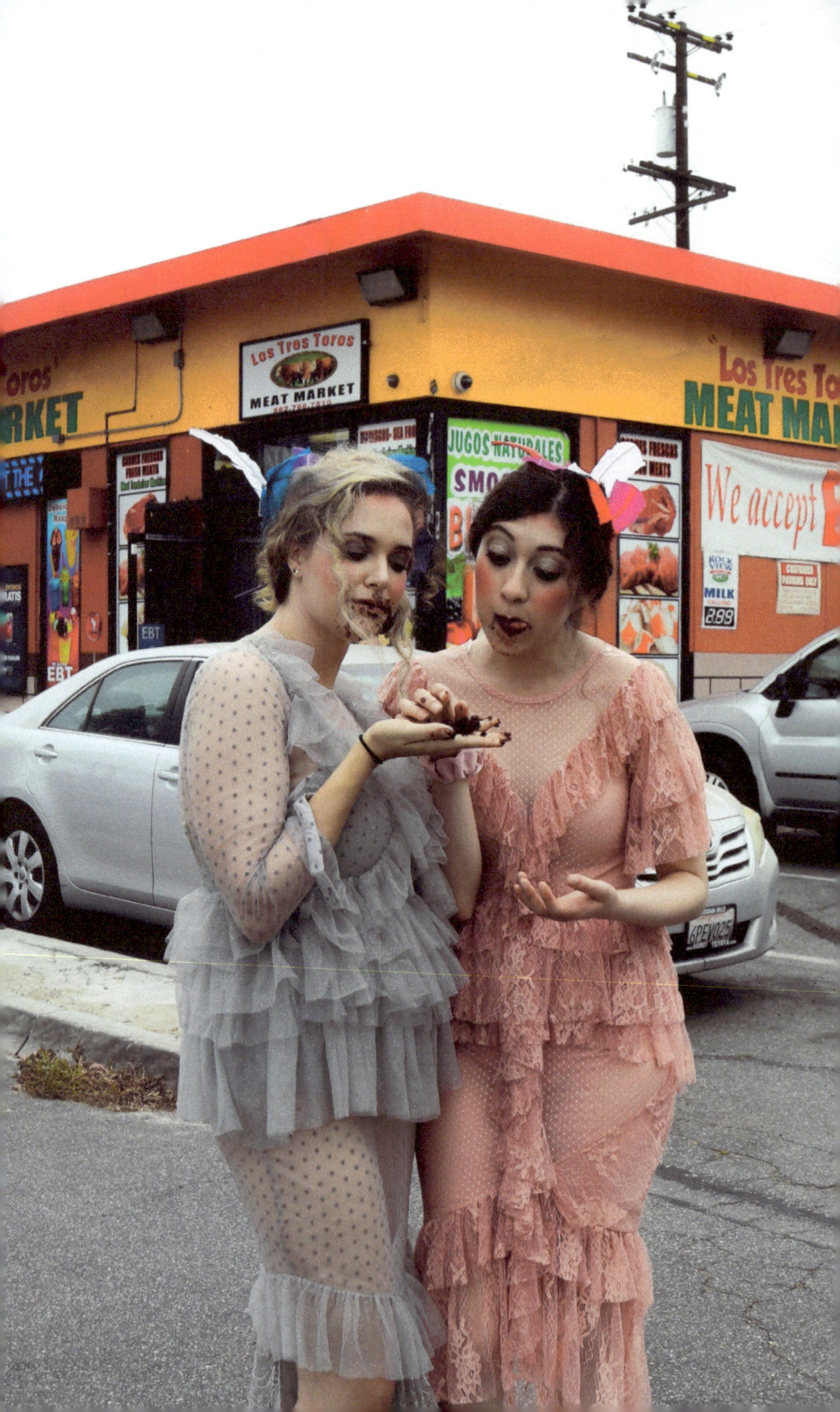

THE SHIT THEY ROT IN

BRENDA HERNÁNDEZ JAIMES

Empty are the people that are ashamed of who they are. These people live in a constant hell without knowing it. To deny and be ashamed of your background, heritage, language that you speak and, ultimately, of your physical appearance is to abandon yourself and leave your soul dry.

Hate has never truly dwelled in my heart, but these hollow people come so very close to creating this feeling. For many years I could never comprehend why anyone would twist their mouth in annoyance when I spoke to them in Spanish.

Speaking in this beautiful language is my way of connecting to my community. To utter a buenos días, provecho or hasta luego is to communicate that I am also like them: a proud Latina and that they aren't alone in this country. This is my way of demonstrating that I'm here as well, with them and I would be there for them. By speaking in my parents native tongue, I create a safe space for my community and I. The chains of having to speak only in broken English are gone and a warmth is quickly surrounding us. This warmth is a small but strong link between us. This link creates a connection and an open trust that was non-existent before. Jokes, advice and bits and pieces of our private life are shared in these few moments because what else do we have to share but ourselves.

But not everyone accepts this warmth from their people. They hear those words in the language that raised them and they sneer, only offering a disgusted glare that would stab at anyone's heart.

"I don't speak Spanish."

Their words feel like someone pulling at my hair. For so many years I never understood why anyone would stop speaking this gorgeous language, our language. But it doesn't ever really end there. The denial goes as far as betraying their birthplace, being ashamed of their childhood home and striving to be as white as possible.

Why would anyone want to remove their rich culture and history for one that is filled with genocide? Why would you claim a culture that is known for appropriating everything and tries so hard to make it their own, while only ever creating a bastardized version of it?

When they say they don't speak Spanish, they are erasing a part of the foundation that defines them. They're ashamed to speak to people that don't fit into the blond and blue eye appearance they dream of becoming one day, without realizing they never will. They're ashamed of the strength it took for our people to endure the many tribulations caused by the people they so desperately want to become. They're embarrassed of their physical appearance and go as far as to powder their face like Porfirio Díaz. But they'll never look as basic as Lauren or Chad.

It's not all their fault for being ashamed of their culture, not really. The quiet racism that white people have instilled on latinos has resulted in these people becoming arrepentidos. The blame can only be shared with the people they idolize.

The birth of this denial can usually be traced back to a simple phrase: "You shouldn't be speaking in Spanish to your children because you'll confuse them."

Confusion can settle in and instead of fighting back by teaching their children their native tongue, they erase the opportunity to participate in the warmth of their community. In a small way it's easy to understand why they would rather not make their children go through the awful bullying and mistreatment they went through, but our people have endured much more. By speaking another language, more doors are opened for children to grow and connect.

To begin with, it's fair to assume that arrepentidos don't have much love for their heritage when it's so easy for their colonizers to come and tell them to change who they are and quickly sway them to destroy any evidence of what makes them Latino without much thought. The denial goes so far as to make them believe that their home country is just as ignorant as white people paint it to be. Their home becomes a country that has no education and and is so dangerous, you can't step out into the daylight without immediately being shot and killed for no reason at all.

But they keep eating the shit that these close minded white people have given them. They stuff their faces with this mistreatment. They eat it up, all of it, time and time again. At the end of the day this insecurity and this denial, this desire to be part of, excludes them from the diverse and welcoming community that birthed them can only backfire. They will never be white. They'll never be a Chad or a Lauren. The white man will always see them as they truly are, as what they've strived so hard to erase. Once they realize their mistake, it will be too late. The people they left behind won't need them, want them, accept them anymore. Mistreatments cannot be forgotten, much less the embarrassment. Instead of being greeted with open arms, the backs of the people who fought for them will be the only thing they see. There will be nothing left for them but to keep ignoring the vile smell of shit that emanates from their mouths. They've let part of who they are die, what else can it do but rot?

EDITORIAL SHOOT
Models: Brenda Hernández Jaimes & Haleigh Bowers
Photographer: Josephine Jael Jimenez
Stylist: Brenda Hernández Jaimes & Josephine Jael Jimenez
Makeup: Josephine Jael Jimenez

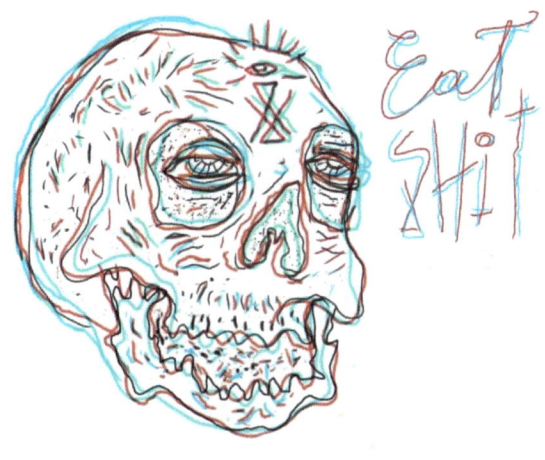

Eat Shit
Digital CX *by Bad Shit*

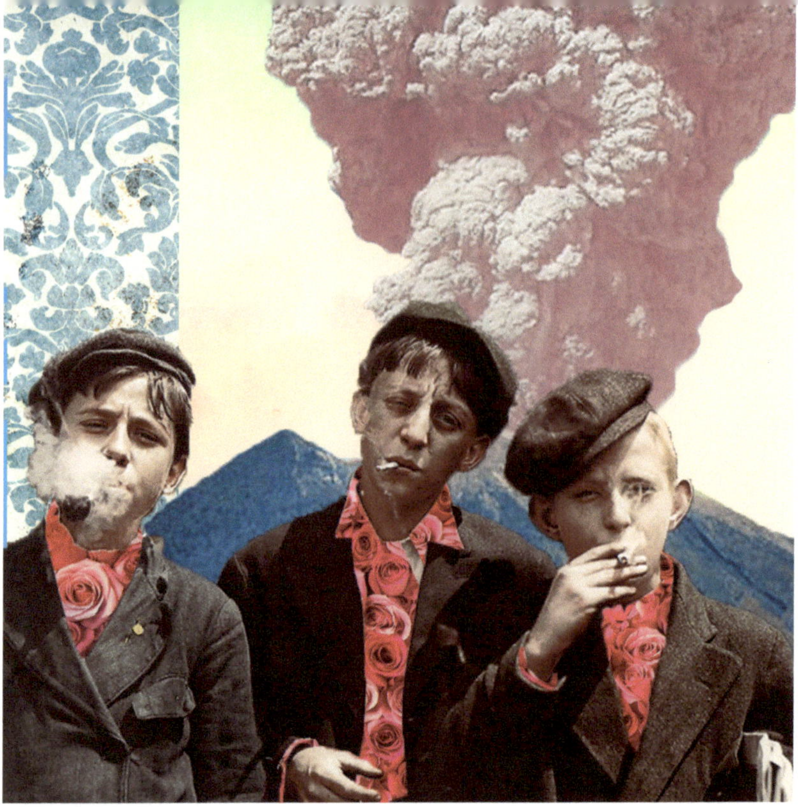

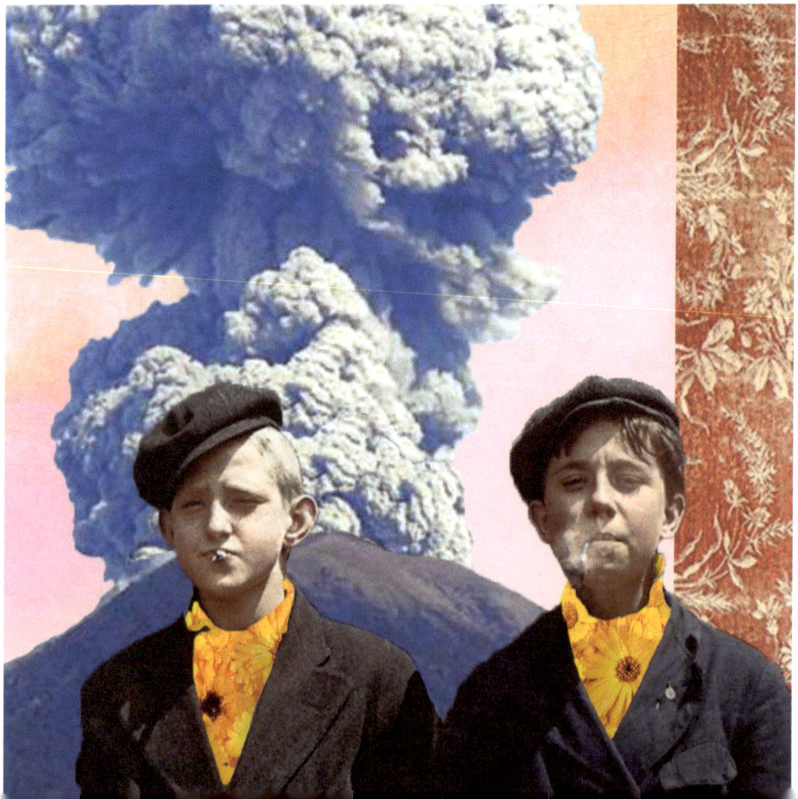

CRACKED

JOSEPH A. REYES

A square jaw,
a cleft chin,
hair that does whatever its owner wants:
an image of perfection.
Perfection created by those who crafted that image
by looking in the mirror,
those who managed to overrule
and inferiorize folx to believe
that their existence was imperfect,
that their skin full of melanin is a defect,
that their deep, chocolate brown eyes
cannot see as clearly or as pure as the sensitive-to-light,
crystal blue.
That their thick, textured hair is "untamable,"
"unmanageable,"
"unprofessional."
That their curvacious bodies
were only meant for sexual objectification
and manipulation.

Fuuuuuuuuuuck your standards of perfection and beauty,
Your lack of rhythm and absence of deep kin still show.
Your mirror is cracked.
7,000,000 years of bad luck to make up for your bullshit.
This regularly scheduled programming is cancelled,
unrenewed,
and shelved until further notice.
Time to sit.

The fuck.

Down.

Light Up & Light Up 2
Digital collages *by Evan Black*

HIS PEOPLE

B. A. DESHAZER

God has to be brown, I smirk and think to myself. His son was brown. Mary and Joseph were brown. His people that He looked after were brown. All biblical stories were about brown people. He only spoke of brown people! If He made man in His own image and His people are brown then God has to be brown. I take a sip, grit my teeth, and breathe as the world swirls around me.

I'm a Latino pastor at a newly founded church. The church is less than a year old and it has already been plagued with hate crimes. It feels like everyday we are scrubbing or painting racial slurs off the sides of the church. Words like "beaners," "Go back to Mexico," or "Church isn't for cholos." The other day they added a new word to their vocabulary: "Wetback." Clever, haven't heard that one before.

I am a devoted husband and a loving father of one, but my wife is off sleeping with her white coworker while our son is in the hospital living off borrowed time. She thinks I'm spineless for not standing up to the cops who just "let these things happen." If I'm being honest,, there's just no reasoning with them, they're only interested in protecting the white people.

Why is this happening to me? What good is it to be a faithful husband, pastor, and father if it this shit gets thrown on you?. 'Blessed are the meek for they shall inherit the earth.' Am I supposed to want to inherit an earth that has been corrupted by white people?

The alcohol overcomes me. Jesus suffered tremendously, through persecution, ridicule, and death. My head spins and my eyes close Nowadays people of color are the ones suffering. They're the ones going through persecution, ridicule, and death. They're the ones being gunned down based on ignorance and circumstance/ They're the ones being belittled and discriminated against. My eyes widen with rage. They work 10 times harder than their white counterparts for things white people barely have to lift a finger for. I tilt my glass back and forth. I've worked so hard to get this church to be part of the community. My pastors keep getting harassed by the cops in the city. The white, good for nothing cops. Well, I guess 'good for only white people' cops. I take another drink. None of the white churches in this neighborhood get this treatment.

If humans are to be Christ-like and if Christ went through great trial and tribulation, then I believe people of color are truly God's people. Another gulp. Our people go through torment every day. White people can't be children of God, can they?. I took another swig of the brown liquor and waited for the calm to overcome me. Suddenly I hear a voice to my left.

"Yes, you are right," he responded with a sly smile in his voice. I slowly turned to a white man in an expensive blue pinstripe suit. He had bright green eyes like a garden, blonde hair slicked back, a strong tall stature.. He sipped what appeared to be a martini; classy, like his image. It was almost as if there was one light in the bar focused directly on him. How long has he been there? Was he talking to me? Was I saying all this out loud? I look him up and down. He was strikingly handsome, poised, and had an intimidating presence about him. He takes another sip and I try to figure him out. Who is he?

He looks back at me and I'm startled at being caught staring. I try to relax, "I'm right?" I retort.

He chuckles and says, "It's funny how humans make the strongest arguments when their mind is the weakest." Did he say... humans?

"Most of the time they are correct, sometimes they are not," he states in playful manner waving his glass around, "but you, my good sir, are correct. White people are different. Pick any white person in here and I will show you."

I look at him puzzled. What's going on?

"C'mon, shouldn't be that hard. There's tons of white people in the world. They definitely outnumber you people in this country, so there should be a plethora to choose from in here." My brow furrows, my face feels red, and I clench my fists.

"Easy there buddy," he says looking at me up and down from the corner of his eye, "I'm kinda protected you know. One false move and it will be 'local gang member raises chaos in quiet bar against well loved community member' in the headlines."

I hate how right he is. Hitting him will make me feel better, but a brown and a white person in a fight, I will always lose when it comes to justice.

"C'mon," he throws his arm around me and turns me to the rest of the bar. My eyes automatically are drawn to a white woman in a bright blue dress in the middle of the bar sitting alone. "Ah, so you found one," he says coyly. "She is definitely a looker, I mean every white person is." My brow furrows at his statement and I try to pull away but his arm tightens around my shoulders holding me in place. "Relax. I am trying to make a point, and let's be honest, you've been in worse situations than this," he leans in closer to whisper, "and you have no better place to run off to, pastor." I shudder. My whole body stiffens and eyes widen. He knows me?

He begins holding his hand outwardly in the woman's direction,

"Now, as I was saying. Look how her porcelain skin glimmers even in the darkest of settings," he says in a soft melodic voice. "Her hair shines bright like the warm golden sun. Her eyes are the most coveted color in the world. Her long legs brings her stature high above everyone else so that she may look down upon them," his eyes darken and he smiles. "She is the model image throughout centuries. No one like her will have her features. Her image can never be obtained unless they are," he pauses as if to say something else but continues, "'cut from the same cloth' so to speak." He waves his hand about as he speaks. I looked at him puzzled trying to figure out what he is saying. "But we are all God's people," I rejoin trying to salvage any malice I have against them and be the 'good' pastor I was meant to be. He raises his eyebrow and scoffs.

He leans in closer resting on one elbow and his drink in the other hand raised. With a dramatic, dark, and roarous voice, "Do you think God's people would dismantle and uproot thousands of civilizations for their own selfish gain? Do you think His people would capture, rape, enslave, and kill people just because they looked different? Do you think God's people would treat the different looking ones like wild beasts? People who put full effort in completely eradicating cultures and create a diaspora within people and families with no remorse? You say we are all God's people, but the only part of God they want anything to do with was creating all of this malevolence in His name," he snorts, "as if to mock Him."

He takes another sip of his martini and softens his tone, "after all of this, they will still take what little culture you have left to celebrate with and mock you. They have taken those aspects of culture and claimed it for themselves: food trucks, taco tuesday, cinco de drinko, the list goes on and on." He smiles proudly, "who else would deny 'white privilege' but still unapologetically reap the benefits of it, all the while constantly watching people of color suffer in their gain. Certainly not God's people."

He leans back and takes another sip of his martini. "God," he snorted, "so in love with his creation. It is uncanny how much you people are like him; full of grace, patience, and kindness." He leans in rapidly swinging his drink toward me, "I mean you people will never rise up against whites!" He laughs in an uproar, "No matter how your numbers grow, no matter the resources, no matter how much shit they put you through. Hell! How much they've put you through already."

His laugh calms, "You can't, you won't and you never will." He tosses back his drink and starts, "and you know why?" He puts his hand on my shoulder and I instantly get a chill of his sinister presence, an unsafe and unwelcomed touch. He seems to have lost his glimmer completely. "Because you are God's people. You are already claimed by God," he answers in a soft tone.

He gracefully descends from his chair, stands tall and erect, and buttons up his coat, "He made man in his image. His people good like Him," he steps closer the white man next to him and grabs his cheeks, "white people are... well... they are like me," he ominously beams back at me. The man doesn't respond, as if he can't feel the suited man's touch. Does he know he's there?

The beauteous man strolled away without another word into the light of the world as his figure darkened against the sunlight. I gazed after him with such awe, with disgust in the pit of my stomach...

"and no wonder, for even Satan disguises himself as an angel of light."
(2 Corinthians 11:14)

UNTITLED

SPENCER C. RICKMAN

Unused yet spend,
crumbling at the lightest touch,
shrouded in the dust
colored sheet of wasted time.
A canvas
upon which to paint a story.
Is this a tragedy
or just a dark comedy?

UNTITLED
Photograph *by Spencer C. Rickman*

LOVE IN THE AGE OF CONVENIENCE

EVAN BLACK

I'm here

                                            You're there.

Until you want to be here.
Here where I am.

                                  But you're still here.

And I asked if I could join.

I'm here,
                            But I could be here.
                            But you said, "no."

So I wait.

And wait.

And I just know you'll join me.
Because you said you would.

But I've been here for a while now.
And I feel a bit used.
It seems you only come to my side
When you

                                  Need something.
                                    Please?

FAKE GRASS BABE
M.

Dear [name redacted],

I cannot be your fake grass babe.

I half expected the trailer from Pleasantville to start playing as we walked through the neighborhood and you told me your dream house included plastic grass.

A few weeks later, your grip tightened across my shoulders and your eyes swam through me.

I cannot be your fake grass babe.

Truth be told, all the succulents on my porch are dead. But when I am ready, I will bring new flowers home and water them.

My mother tells me that a garden grows better with fertilizer. It's too bad you couldn't handle shit.

- M

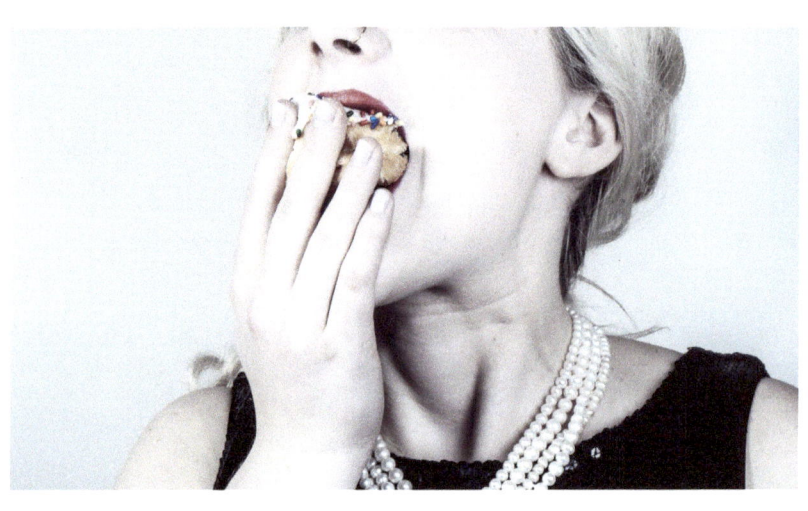
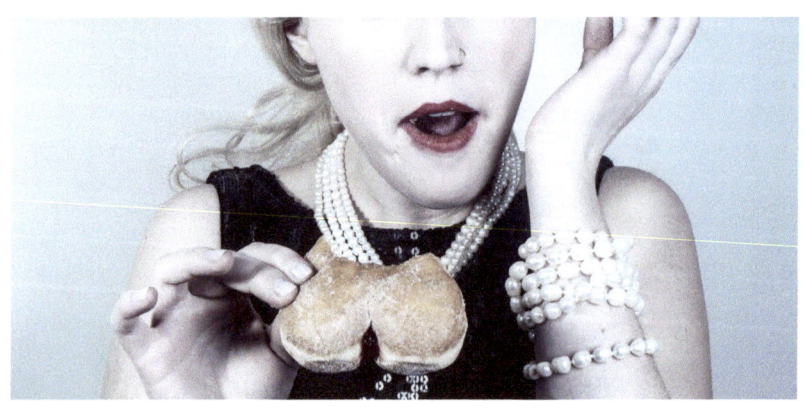

> sometimes
> I cry
> because the
> fight seems
> like a lost
> cause,
> but then I
> remember the
> words of my father:
> "they've never
> wanted us here
> and still we remain."

ANCHOR BABY
Ink on paper *by Josephine Jael Jimenez*

UNTITLED
Photograph *by Natalie Galante*

Dinners

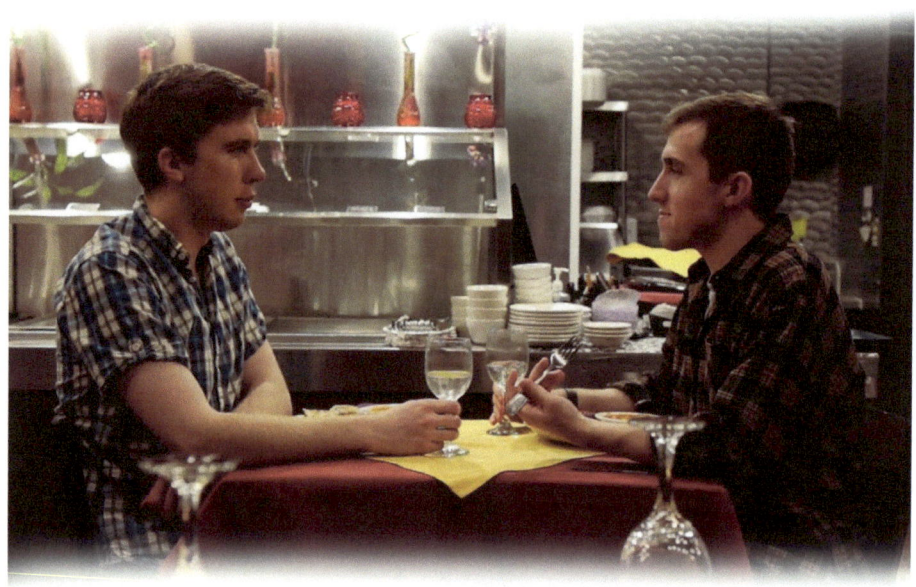

Drew & Logan

Starring
Stephen Miller & Aaron Wesselman

Written by Stephen Miller			Directed by Jacob Ortega

DINNERS: DREW & LOGAN

STEPHEN MILLER

Drew & Logan is among other things a story of mismatched expectations, and how modern dating app culture sets us up for disappointment. Particularly in the gay community, the incongruity between those looking for something real and those simply looking for a casual hookup often leads to chasms of loneliness between young gay men. Or, in the case of both Drew and Logan, they settle for the casual hookup experience in the end because their hopes for a deeper connection are dashed, and that fleeting moment of stimulation they agree to is the easiest band-aid fix for the human connection they yearn for.

The short also tries to take a candid look at the pervasiveness of sexual assault in all walks of life. In particular, we wanted to explore the fact that when men are the victims of sexual assault, their experiences are generally minimized by others. The idea of a man being sexually assaulted is so foreign to most people, including Drew, that our minds aren't even able to process the information before us. Drew laughs at Logan's story not because he thinks it's funny, but because he has no framework to understand what Logan went through, and the easiest way to defuse that resulting tension is through laughter.

TRACK TWO.
A BEAT BY WILL HAWKINS

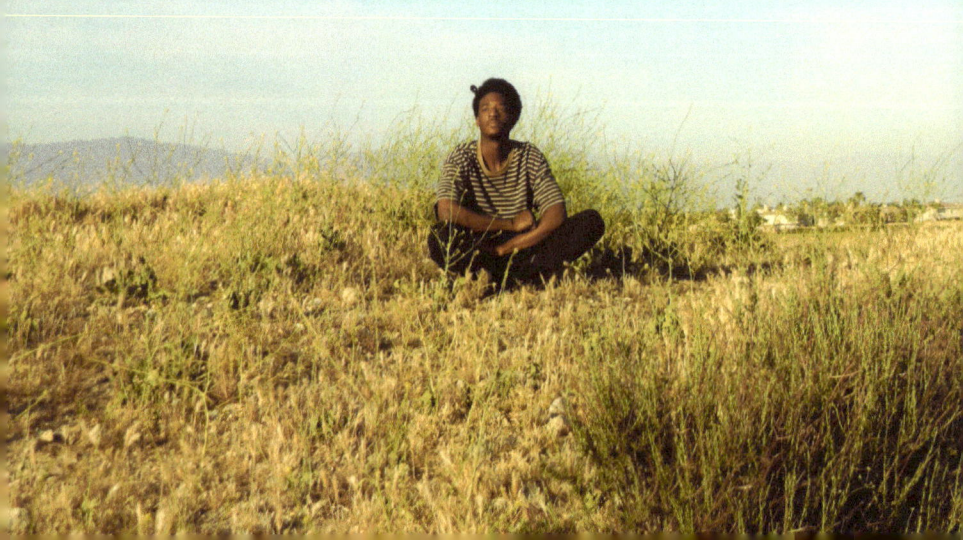

PARA MI MAMÁ
Y MI ABUELA

REBEKAH C. GUERRA

My mother was born in Santo Domingo, Dominican Republic, the oldest daughter of five siblings. Her parents were part of the working class, her father was a day laborer, and her mother a homemaker and teacher.

Three years before she was born, the long-standing military dictator of the Dominican Republic, Rafael Trujillo, was assassinated on the road to the country's capital. He was driving a blue 1957 Chevrolet Bel Air - an American convertible muscle car - when he was ambushed, shot and killed.

The irony of the American car is not lost on me. In fact, it was the United States government that enabled Trujillo's rise to power after their 1916 occupation of the Dominican Republic. And, in an ironic twist of fate for Trujillo, it was the CIA who trained the men who killed him on the side of the road - another casualty in the long history of oppressive imperialistic policies enacted by the United States.

Even though Trujillo's demise came in 1961, the legacy of his oppressive regime continues to this day. Trujillo's policies of state terrorism - particularly against Haiti and those of Haitian descent - tainted the cultural landscape of the Dominican Republic. Haitians were associated with poverty, disease, and filth - their dark skin a testament to the sins they allegedly committed against Dominicans. Even in a country where over two-thirds of the population is mixed race, descendants of African slaves and their European oppressors, anti-blackness and colorism is still prevalent. As recently as the mid-2010s, Dominicans of Haitian descent were threatened with statelessness and deportation, echoing Trujillo's early 20th Century ethnic cleansing policies. Discrimination against Haitians is by far the Dominican Republic's greatest cultural sin.

▲▲▲

Born and raised in the post-Trujillo era, my mother grew up hearing stories of her parents' experiences as an ostensibly mixed-race couple: her father, a dark-skinned Haitian descendant, and her mother, a light-skinned woman with blue eyes, and a descendant of British Virgin Islanders.

My abuela, although raised in the Dominican Republic, spoke the language of the colonizers, growing up in a bilingual home. Although my grandmother was born into relative privilege, the daughter of highly educated parents, she effectively abdicated her higher class status by marrying a black man. As a result, my grandmother and her children were targeted in the Trujillo regime. She would tell my mother stories of hiding the older children under a mattress when the military men came into the neighborhood, their dark skin and light eyes a testament to the racial admixture that Trujillo reviled. No physical harm ever came to pass the family, but the mental scars were evident - the message, simply stated, was that they were second-class citizens. That message, combined with the reality of working-class poverty and a struggle to put food on the table, contributed to the generational trauma from which the family has never truly recovered.

My grandmother was a fierce protector of her family, unwavering in her dedication to keeping her children safe, and encouraging their education in an effort to provide them with a better life. Her eyes, bright and shining, belie a dark past of pain and struggle, oppression and discrimination, all a result of her choice to "lower herself" to marry a dark-skinned man. I like to believe that she has never regretted surrendering her privilege. Her five children gave her purpose and meaning in the midst of the storm of a dictatorship determined to punish her for her decision.

▲▲▲

I posit that Trujillo's oppression of Haitians stemmed from a deep ignorance of the dynamics of race and class. Haiti's own history of abject poverty, an apparent punishment for revolting against their powerful French oppressors, influenced Trujillo's ideology. The race and class status of the Haitian people is inextricably linked - for Trujillo, this meant that their poverty and blackness are synonymous. The cursed mark of dark skin, the desperation of poverty, and the legacy of class struggle against the White ruling class were all contributing factors to Trujillo's plan for complete ethnic cleansing, a set of policies that came to a climax during el corte - the Parsley Massacre of over 35,000 Haitians. Antihaitianismo was at its worst during that time, a true hatred of everything Haitian - their language, culture, customs, and religion.

▲▲▲

My mother, with her dark skin, nappy hair, and thick Dominican accent, immigrated to the U.S. in 1984. She was sponsored by a wealthy aunt and uncle who saw her potential for great things, and paid for her plane ticket to Washington, D.C. to attend university. Throughout her undergraduate experience, she worked as many as three jobs at a time - walking dogs, cleaning bathrooms, and doing hair - while studying English at night at the Smithsonian Institution's museums in D.C. She graduated with a Bachelor's in Business Administration, a tribute to the work her mother invested in her to get a quality education. Her pride in walking across the stage to receive her diploma was in honor of the legacy of my grandmother - strong, determined, and resolute. My mother was free of the influence of Trujillo, free from the oppression of an anti-black culture that was determined to be rid of her.

Equipped with the knowledge of her education, my mother went on to become an executive in a sports organization, working her way up from her initial role as a secretary. Her tenacity and innate drive to prove her worth - perhaps a remnant of a childhood where she was seen as culturally worthless - spurred her on to success in her career.

My mother is an incredible woman. She is determined, self-sacrificing, and hard-working, stubborn and unwavering in her dedication to those she loves. Her mother's legacy of dedication to her children continues on in her every word and action. She was able to repay her mother's own selfless dedication, sponsoring her to come to the United States in the mid-90's. My mother is constantly seeking to improve the lives of others around her, often putting aside her own needs in favor of those around her. I have an eternal gratitude for her fortitude.

▲▲▲

Rafael Trujillo was assassinated on May 30, 1961. Three years later, my mother was born. Her mother carried her for nine months, toiling through labor and childbirth to bring about an amazing life, still bearing the emotional scars of the pain Trujillo brought upon the Dominican and Haitian people. Nevertheless, my abuela persisted, as did my mother after her. I like to think of their strength in the face of adversity as a protest against Trujillo's legacy of oppression and cruelty, their own silent struggle to make a better life for themselves against all odds. Their tenacity is their legacy.

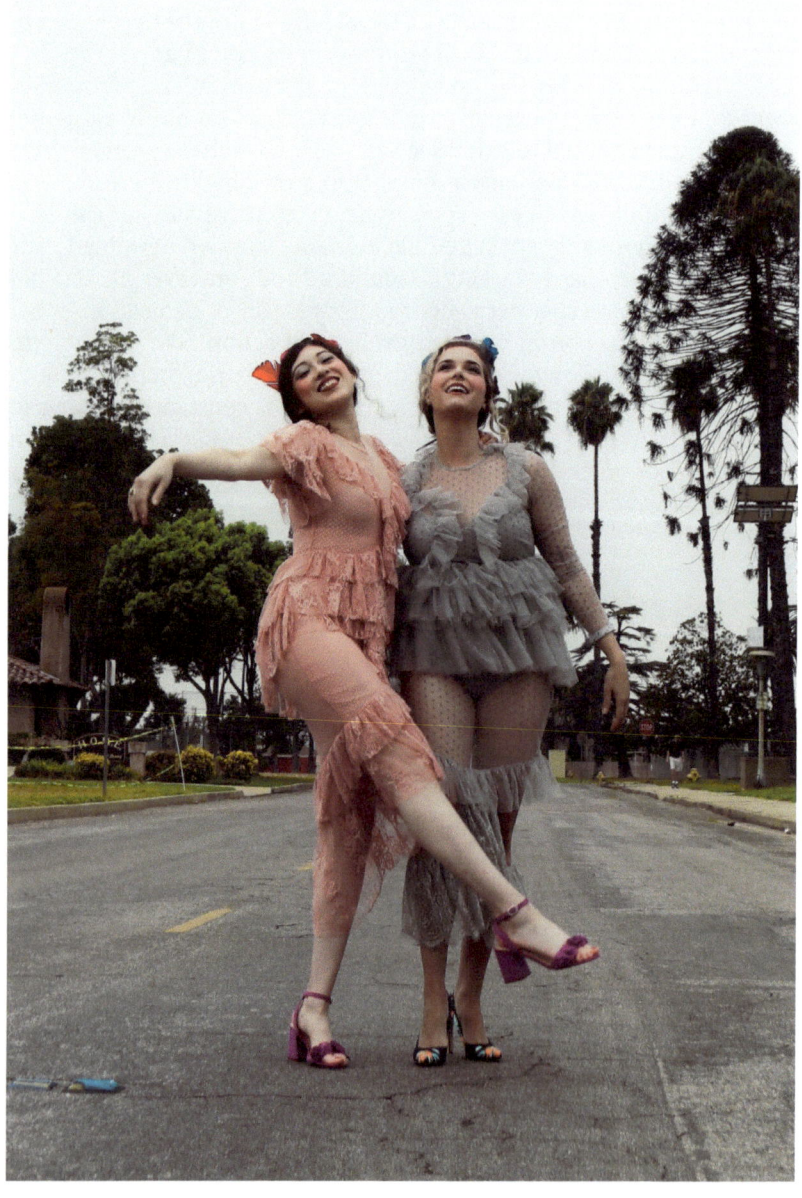

PRETTY PEOPLE DIE IN LA

JOSEPHINE JAEL JIMENEZ

    Where do all the pretty people go when they want to die? Some say LA, some say New York. I've even heard they just disappear altogether because you have to be ugly to die the way humans do.
    I've seen enough pretty faces in this city to know that maybe some people are right. This City of Angels is where the closest thing to heavenly beings come to find the end because there's no place like it to torture your soul towards it.
    Sitting in hours of traffic and paying way too much money for real estate can drive any sane human being to the brink of existence, but pretty people even more so. They could go anywhere in the world and be beautiful, but instead they find themselves in a sea of people that look just like them or nothing like them. Without even knowing it, they drove themselves right to the source of pain and comparison that will probably be their downfall because pretty people don't live in LA. They just die here.
    Maybe not physically at first, but emotionally and mentally. Maybe not even all at once, but slowly slowly slowly they realize that this city of lights and glamour and Hollywood feeds off of people like them, people that only exist to be pretty.
    It's like a curse we're all too aware of, but don't care enough to move away from. Oh, but us ugly people are safe from harm. We don't have to worry about dying in this city because this city is ours and it loves us. We built it with our hands and we carved its meaning with our voices. Ugly people may die here eventually, but they die cradled in the arms of mother Los Angeles. Our souls flow down the San Gabriel River to the horizon stretched out before Long Beach. This city knows who has loved her well and who has loved her dearly.
    But to my beautiful friends in my beautiful city, don't worry about the dying. Even in death, my city is sweet. She will treat you to a wonderful downward spiral. No, you many never be ugly and you may never survive within her borders, but you will never feel death creeping into your pores. It will not be painful. One day, if you're smart, you'll realize you weren't made for her and you will choose to leave, only to visit when you miss the feeling of her arms wrapped around your neck. But even if you choose to stay, do not be

afraid. Life will be wild and lovely despite the torture. It's a love so toxic and so sweet, like the scent of almonds wafting up from cyanide.

    Don't try to understand. There is no understanding why the ugly will always prevail here, not if you're beautiful. But here's a taste, for torture's sake: Beautiful people come to this city and think they deserve her love more than those who have come before them, more than the ugly people who have been here all along. LA knows who has been good to her. LA knows who truly loves her for all that she has been, is, and can be. To live and die in LA is a privilege only she can grant you. Welcome.

THE ANSWER TO THE PROBLEM

JOSE CORDOVA

they used to come at night
boots stomping
glass shattering
red fireflies at our chests
their mechanical tornadoes above

many of us were taken
bit by bit
sometimes they came back beaten
or in plastic bags
some just disappeared

one day
it was one too many

it was the day we woke up
it was the day we all saw the same thing
we were all victims
to this social disease
it was the day the collective anger
pointed not at each other
but in the proper direction

and the neighborhoods
and the hoods
and the people
all rose up

in a few days
years happened

we surround the precincts
we surround their offices
we surround city hall

and now they have a problem

and we all sing
and we all dance
and we all build
together

OUR PEOPLE

BAD SHIT
@bad_shit
fb.com/okreskate.rodriguez

JOSEPHINE JAEL JIMENEZ
@josietakestheworld
josietakestheworld.com

B. A. DESHAZER
@bee.andi

LEX BROWN
@lexlbrown

BRENDA HERNÁNDEZ JAIMES
@bren_jai
brenjai.com

M.
an anonymous contributer

DINNERS
@dinners_series
fb.com/dinnersseries

NATALIE GALANTE
nataliegalante.com

EVAN BLACK
@evanisthenewblack
evanvblack.com

REBEKAH C. GUERRA
rebekahguerra.com

HALEIGH BOWERS
@haleighbowers

SPENCER C. RICKMAN
@sprencer

JOSE CORDOVA
@wrdspektor

STEPHEN MILLER
@millertime141

JOSEPH A. REYES
@joeykangarooooo

WILL HAWKINS
@willhawk.beats

YOUNG IGNORANTES
@youngignorantes
youngignorantes.com

www.ingramcontent.com/pod-product-compliance
Lightning Source LLC
Chambersburg PA
CBHW040342220526
45473CB00009B/2766